Mean Behind the Screen

WHAT YOU NEED TO KNOW ABOUT CYBERBULLYING

by Toney Allman

Content Adviser:
Billy AraJeJe Woods, Ph.D.,
Department of Psychology, Saddleback College,
Mission Viejo, California

Reading Adviser:
Alexa L. Sandmann, Ed.D.,
Professor of Literacy, College and Graduate School
of Education, Health and Human Services,
Kent State University

Compass Point Books
151 Good Counsel Drive
P.O. Box 669
Mankato, MN 56002-0669

This book was manufactured with paper containing
at least 10 percent post-consumer waste.

Photographs ©: Capstone Press/Karon Dubke, cover ; Landov LLC/
Bloomberg News/Kimberly White, 6, PA Photos/Danny Lawson, 27; Alamy/
PSL Images, 7, Ronnie McMillan, 8, axel leschinski, 41; Shutterstock/Monkey
Business Images, 9, Mandy Godbehear, 10, Stephen Coburn, 21; iStockphoto/
Laurence Gough, 13, Ben Blankenburg, 29; PhotoEdit Inc./John Neubauer, 15,
Billy E. Barnes, 30; Getty Images Inc./Taxi/Ulrik Tofte, 17, Stone/Bruce Ayres,
38; 123RF/Alex Hinds, 18; Newscom, 23; Corbis/Ed Kashi, 25, Jim Craigmyle,
34; AP Images/John Russell, 26, Jacqueline Larma, 32.

For Compass Point Books
Brenda Haugen, Heidi Thompson, Jo Miller, LuAnn Ascheman-Adams,
Joe Ewest, Nick Healy, and Catherine Neitge

For Bow Publications
Bonnie Szumski, Kim Turner, and Katy Harlowe

Library of Congress Cataloging-in-Publication Data
  Allman, Toney.
Mean behind the screen : what you need to know about cyberbullying /
by Toney Allman.
     p. cm.—(What's the Issue?)
  Includes index.
  ISBN 978-0-7565-4145-3 (library binding)
1. Cyberbullying—Juvenile literature. I. Title. II. Series.
  HV6773.A43 2009
  302.3—dc22   2008039484

Visit Compass Point Books on the Internet at *www.compasspointbooks.com*
or e-mail your request to *custserv@compasspointbooks.com*

TABLE OF CONTENTS

CHAPTER one

BULLIES IN ACTION

Chances are that you've been bullied once or twice in your life. Or that you've seen a bully in action. If so, you know that bullying is mean. And it hurts. And now there's a new kind of bullying out there. It's done over the Internet or by cell phone. It's called cyberbullying.

It isn't pretty. Cyberbullying is any kind of text messaging, instant messaging (IMing), e-mail, or posting that is meant to frighten, harass, or embarrass the receiver.

From Dissing to Danger

Cyberbullies get their kicks by scaring, embarrassing, teasing, or shaming their victims. This can mean putting someone down, posting embarrassing facts or photos, threatening physical harm, or betraying secrets.

Dissing someone online is one form of cyberbullying, says therapist Nancy Willard, an expert on cyberbullying. That's when someone sends or posts rumors or gossip about someone else. Sometimes the bully even invites other people to join in and add more nasty messages. And they don't just do it once. They keep doing it over and over again. Examples of this are all too common. One teen talked about a guy in her class who was bullied on MySpace. She explained: "He's like the smart kid in class. Everybody's jealous. They all want to be smart. ... And some girl in my class started this I Hate [Guy's Name] MySpace thing. So everybody in school goes on it to comment bad things about this boy."

Cyberbullying is also about invading someone's privacy. The Center for Responsible Internet Use tells of one such instance of cyberbullying. Greg* was overweight and in high school. One day he was changing his

You Call These Friends?

Experts define cyberbullying as harassment between two or more people. It happens most often with people who know each other at school. Cyberbullying goes by different names. Cyberbullying is the biggie, but sometimes it's called cyber abuse, electronic aggression, Internet harassment, or Internet bullying. Whatever you call it, it's all basically the same thing. When the bullying is between cyber friends on blogs or at social networking sites, the people usually don't know each other in real life. But since these sites are communities, the victim's Internet social life and cyber friendships can be destroyed. People may say, "Kids will be kids," or "It's a part of growing up." But experts don't agree. They say people are damaged by cyberbullying.

* In this book, names have been changed to protect the privacy of people involved, except in cases where names were reported in the media.

Information travels quickly on the Internet. It doesn't take long for embarrassing pictures or stories to get passed along.

clothes in the locker room at school, and another teen named Matt secretly took a photo of him with a cell phone. Then Matt sent the embarrassing picture to his friends in class. These friends had forwarded it to more friends before Greg had even left the locker room. By the time he was dressed, kids all over the school were laughing at him.

Cyberbullies have even been known to reveal people's innermost secrets to the whole world. And sometimes it has dire consequences. Shaquille Wisdom confided that he was gay to a kid he thought he could trust. Turns out the so-called friend wasn't a friend at all. He blabbed Shaquille's secret all over the place. And then other students posted the information on their Web sites and taunted him even more. Shaquille killed himself after his secret came to light.

Because cyberbullies mess with other kids' feelings to try to scare or hurt them or push them around, cyberbullying can be dangerous. Close to half of teens who hang out on social networking sites such as MySpace and Facebook say they've been cyberbullied.

Sometimes the bullying is more than teasing or name-calling. It can get pretty aggressive. More than 10 percent of kids who've been bullied say

Millions of Victims

Cyberbullying is not just some freak thing. About one-third of American teens, or 13 million young people, say they've been cyberbullied. A study found that girls are more likely than boys to be targets of cyberbullying. Thirty-eight percent of the girls surveyed said they had been bullied online, and 26 percent of the boys said they'd been targeted by a cyberbully. Girls between the ages of 15 and 17 were most likely of all to report being cyberbullied (41 percent). But 12- to 14-year-old girls ran a close second (34 percent).

In June 2008, Facebook attracted 132 million unique visitors, while MySpace attracted 118 million.

they've been threatened, and half of those say they were scared for their safety.

Willard tells of one guy who was angry at his girlfriend for breaking up with him. He posted a picture of her at an online site where people talked about sex. He gave the whole discussion group her e-mail address and cell phone number. Any creeps who wanted to could have found out where she lived and gone after her. It didn't happen—this time. Sometimes, though, cyber-bullying spreads throughout the Internet and is almost impossible to stop.

No Escape

Kylie knows this firsthand. And it's an experience she never, ever wants to repeat. One morning at school, a classmate told Kylie about a new Web site. It was called "Kill Kylie Incorporated." Its purpose, it said, was "to show people how gay Kylie Kenney is." And it added, "Kylie must die." Kylie was shocked. She

Threatening someone can lead to serious consequences, including loss of Internet or cell phone privileges and even arrest.

Cyberbullying can lead to teasing and bullying in person, too.

had no idea who would do this or why. And it just kept getting worse. Someone began IMing other girls at Kylie's school. Using Kylie's screen name, the messages asked them out on dates. Kylie says, "I was just so ashamed, humiliated, and scared. I couldn't understand why anyone would do this."

Kylie didn't know what to do. She told her parents, and they went to the police. The police immediately killed the Web site. And they tracked down the cyberbullies—two boys at her school who had put up the Internet site and stolen Kylie's online identity. But for Kylie, it was too late.

"I was just so ashamed, humiliated, and scared. I couldn't understand why anyone would do this."

The cyberbullying took on a life of its own. Everywhere at school, kids pointed and laughed at Kylie. It seemed as if everyone in her school had seen the Web site, and now they were joining in and acting like

9

it was all great fun. Suddenly Kylie had no friends. Kylie said, "I had no escape."

Kylie's parents switched her to a new school, but it didn't help. The kids had all seen the Web site. Kylie was teased again. And then she started getting more embarrassing e-mails and threatening cell phone calls. It seemed as if the whole world had turned against Kylie—like she was an object of fun, instead of a real person. Finally her parents took her out of school. Home schooling was her only escape.

Too Much to Bear

Although Kylie's cyberbullies were caught, that's not often the case. According to studies, almost half of cyberbullies hide their identities. And it's easy to do that on the Web. In the anonymous world of cyberspace, bullies rarely have to come face to face with their victims. Cyberbullies don't have to be strong to bully. Anyone can play tough hiding behind a personal computer or cell phone.

The other big difference is that their bullying is out there for everyone to see. With just a few mouse clicks, a cruel attack can become very public. This is what happened to Ryan Halligan. He'd been bullied at school for years. When the cyberbullying began, it was the last straw. Ryan had

Cyberbullying victims often feel anxious and suffer from low self-esteem.

I've Heard About That

Lots of tweens and teens know that cyberbullying is going on at their schools. Here's what some had to say about it:

- "My best friend in middle school, she had a Xanga [social networking page] and someone posted this horrible one about her. It was dedicated to her."
- "I have heard of people knowing someone's password and going in and changing their MySpace."
- "I've heard of people going into chat rooms and picking on one person."
- "I know someone who posted pictures of different people and they were just making fun of them."
- "I know someone who got mean text messages."
- "At my old school there was some kind of comment thing where all these kids ganged up on (a girl). It wasn't really a blog site, just a comment Web site."

connected online with a popular girl from school. He spent hours IMing her, sharing his private thoughts and feelings. To the girl and her friends, it was all a joke. They passed around his IMs and laughed. Ryan was already depressed. When he found out what they were doing, he killed himself.

Cyberbullying doesn't always end that way. But it does make people feel depressed, frightened, hurt, and lonely. Cyberbullying can make you feel so awful you even start to wonder what's wrong with you. But hear this: It's never your fault if it happens to you.

CHAPTER two

WHY THEY DO IT

The person who cyberbullies is really the one with the problems. There is no "one size fits all" when it comes to excuses for cyberbullying. Kids make different excuses for doing it. But if you've ever done it, seen it, or been a victim of it, you might already know it's about power, anger, and getting your kicks by hurting others.

Cyberbullying is all about power, the experts say. "Bullying involves a power play; trying to make someone else feel weak and helpless, while inflating your own value," explains Joan E. Lisante, an attorney and expert on Internet laws. So just like schoolyard bullies, cyberbullies feel superior when they can lord it over someone else. Some of them will even brag about their actions, hoping others will admire them.

That's what happened to Tashana when her family moved and suddenly she was the *new* girl at school. Tashana tried to make friends. She tried to get to know some of the popular girls. Cameron was the leader. Tashana learned pretty fast how mean Cameron could be. Cameron and her friends joked about other people's looks, their clothes, and even their religion. When Tashana objected, her new friends turned on her. At first they teased her in person at school. They called her names like "Zit Zilla," "Pimple Face," and "Fish Head." Then the girls posted a Web site about Tashana.

Bully Excuses

Experts try to understand what makes cyberbullies tick. In one Internet survey, more than 1,500 teens were asked about their experiences with cyberbullying. About 17 percent of the teens admitted they had cyberbullied someone. And 50 percent of those said they had cyberbullied just for the fun of it. When asked for other reasons, 22 percent of the cyberbullies said they were teaching their victims something. (Who knows what?) Thirteen percent said being bullied makes the victim "stronger." Forty percent of the cyberbullies believed that online bullying isn't as bad as bullying a person face-to-face.

If you or someone you know is being cyberbullied, tell a trusted adult.

13

It said, "Tashana is a LOSER."
It was full of ugly remarks
and gossip. Cameron and her
friends thought it was hilarious.
Apparently they felt good about
themselves with their put-downs
of Tashana. They entertained
themselves by hurting her.

Malicious Fun

Putting someone else down isn't
always enough for cyberbullies.
Sometimes they also pile on
threats. In Toledo, Ohio, two
teen girls did this on MySpace.
Both girls had MySpace pages,
and they posted messages to
each other about a third girl
they didn't like. They discussed
things like how they were
going to slit the girl's throat
and whether they would smash
her head into the ground. They
joked about hiding the victim's
body after she was dead and
talked about going to prison
together. These girls may have
felt powerful, but that feeling

Whom Do I Bully?

Researchers have tried
to find out which people
cyberbullies are most likely
to attack. In one study, the
bullies reported that they
"bullied another student
at school most frequently,
followed by a friend and
strangers." So, most of the
time, a cyberbully attacks
someone he or she knows
but is not friends with. In
this same study, 11 percent
of the students admitted
to having cyberbullied
someone within the last
two months.

didn't last long. They were dis-
covered, arrested, and convicted
of menacing. A judge sentenced
both girls to probation and 30
hours of community service. The
judge also ordered that they lose
access to MySpace and all IMing
services. The judge ordered
them to write a letter of apology
to their victim. The girls' fami-

If you think you're anonymous on the Internet, think again. If you're caught cyberbullying, you could find yourself in court answering to serious charges.

lies had to pay an undisclosed amount in fines and court costs.

Revenge

Cyberbullying can also be about revenge. Some cyber-bullies think it's their only way to get back at people who were mean to them. Kids who are picked on at school, for instance, might not be able to find a way to fight back. So they turn to the Internet as a way to make the school bul-lies pay without ever having to confront them in real life.

Sometimes kids will seek revenge in a more general way. For example, maybe the jocks at school have bullied an unathletic boy. So he turns against anyone he thinks is a jock. If he meets someone who seems like a jock online or even in another school, he attacks. The cyberbully feels as if he is making all the jocks in the world pay for how he was treated by one of them at his school. Is the chosen victim really a bullying jock? There is no way to know.

With cyberbullying you rarely have to see the other person or deal with your feelings in an upfront way. So cyberbullying for revenge is a cowardly way to take care of your feelings. Revenge feels good in the moment, but hurting someone else to make yourself feel better is a double whammy. You never learn to stand up for yourself, and you're doing the

Old-Fashioned Paper and Pen

Back in your parents' day, there was no Internet, but there were slam books. Students passed around a spiral notebook with a question on each page. There were questions like "Who is the worst-dressed?" or "Who is the fattest girl in our class?" or "Why don't you like _____?" Kids wrote comments anonymously and dissed unpopular people or kids they disliked. Slam books were a form of bullying that really hurt the victims named in the harsh, cruel pages. Today slam books haven't died out. They've just moved to the Internet, where they're more visible than ever before.

same thing to someone else that made you feel bad.

If Your Friends Do ...

As your mother might say, "If

your friend jumped off a bridge, would you do it, too?" The answer, of course, is no. But to some cyberbullying cliques, the group that bullies together stays together. Some kids bully so they can feel they are part of an "in" group. But if you think about it for very long, you real- ize that hanging with a group of friends who bullies puts you in a sketchy situation. It's easy to become the victim of the bullies and be tossed out of your own group. While it may be tempt- ing to get popular by acting superior, it's far better to be popular for being a good friend.

Do you think cyberbullying and teasing others is fun? Try to think about how the victims feel. Would you want to be in their shoes? How do you look through their eyes?

If your friends send hurtful text messages to another friend, what's to stop them from doing the same to you someday? Are these really good friends to have?

Erin learned this the hard way. She was the leader of a clique of bullying girls. Most of the girls were afraid of her, including her friend Michelle. No one dared to cross Erin.

But the power backfired. As the girls grew older, Michelle began to dislike Erin. A rumor started that Erin had tried to hook up with a boy Michelle liked. First Michelle turned on Erin, and then she got a whole group of girls to join her. They flooded Erin's e-mail with angry messages. They shunned her at school. As other students learned of the attacks, people who didn't even know Erin called her ugly names and attacked her online.

Eventually Michelle felt sorry for her actions, but Erin's school life was ruined for years. She had no friends, hated school, and got failing grades because she couldn't concentrate. She said, "I'm such a scared person now. I'm always worried about

> *"I'm such a scared person now. I'm always worried about what people think about me."*

what people think about me. ... I'm always worried about why people hate me. They made me like this now."

Cyberbullies don't stop to think about how the other person feels. And it's oh-so-easy to do that over the Internet. No matter how angry you are, there's no excuse for cyberbullying. When cyberbullies go too far, they can suffer serious consequences, and the person they cyberbullied may be hurt far more than they ever imagined.

CHAPTER three

BUSTED!

Think cyberbullying sounds like fun? Think again. Cyberbullies who get caught can land in big trouble. They can be suspended or kicked out of school, and they can be banned from Internet sites. And if it's a safety thing, they may even be arrested and tried for a crime.

One thing that you ought to know is that you're not *really* anonymous online. You might *feel* like you are. You might *feel* like you're hidden and protected behind your online user name, but you aren't. Thinking you are posting or text messaging anonymously is a big mistake.

Anyone who uses the Internet leaves cyber footprints behind. Everything you do on a computer or a cell phone leaves a permanent record that experts can trace. If you make threats or steal personal information, that's a crime. Police take threats and ID theft seriously. And they can follow your cyber trail if they need to.

You may not see it, but everything you do on the Internet leaves a trail.

They can find out your Internet service provider (ISP) from your e-mail or instant message. They can order the ISP to give them the name and address for your account. The same can be done with cell phones. Think about the legal trouble you could cause for yourself by posting that you're out to get someone. Think about being outed to school authorities. It happens. That power trip could become a nightmare. It's not worth the risk.

But What If I'm Really Mad?

If you're really angry, take a break. Don't respond to mean online comments. Instead, find a way to calm down so you don't do anything you might later regret. Phone a friend, take a bath, or go shoot some hoops. Don't get involved in cyberbullying. Remember, a bully often becomes a target later on. What goes around could easily come back to you.

Get Out and Stay Out

Cyberbullying that doesn't involve threats or the theft of personal information (such as phone numbers and passwords) isn't against the law, but there can still be serious consequences— at school, at home, and on the Web. For one thing, you can be banned from sites when you are reported for cyberbullying. You could lose your IM and ISP account. Using your account to cyberbully is a violation of ISP and IM terms of service at nearly all companies. If you are reported multiple times, the service will suspend your account. It's likely that suspensions will become more common in the future as awareness of cyberbullying grows.

In 2008, both MySpace and Facebook agreed to help state law enforcement groups to improve online safety for kids, including cracking down on cyberbully behaviors. Almost all social networking sites have lists of safety tips and easy ways for users to report abuse or harassment. MySpace even has a cyberbullying hotline. Both sites promise to take every

Where's the Smiley Face?

Don't get someone mad without meaning to. Online, people can't see your face. They can't read your expression and be sure you're joking. In one study, college students were asked to e-mail two messages. One had to be sincere, the other one sarcastic. Senders thought they were obvious and clear 97 percent of the time. But receivers of the messages recognized sarcasm only 84 percent of the time. That meant sometimes they thought a sarcastic message was sincere. And they got hurt or mad. Use emoticons when you send a message. They tell the receiver if you were serious or being funny.

Facebook and MySpace have strict rules against cyberbullying.

report seriously. They investigate any users who violate the site rules, and they will drop people who cyberbully. Site rules on MySpace, for example, include prohibiting anything that is offensive or promotes racism, bigotry, hatred, or physical harm of any kind against any group or individual; anyone who harasses or advocates harassment of another person (meaning repeatedly tormenting someone or urging others to do that); anyone who publicly posts information that poses or creates a privacy or security risk to any person; or anyone who includes a photograph or video of another person that is posted without that person's consent.

Both MySpace and Facebook will delete and shut down inappropriate comments and hate pages. People who participate in a hate group page get kicked out, too.

Cyberbullies also get banned from chat rooms and other online communities. A moderator at one popular gaming forum said he got angry when he saw

Are You Being a Cyberbully?

Are you possibly headed for trouble? Check out some of these questions based on a quiz from Stop Bullying Now:

- Have you gotten someone else to send a hurtful message about somebody you don't like?
- Did you spread or forward a nasty rumor about someone, either online or over the phone?
- Do you and your friends keep someone else from hanging out with you or socializing with you—either online or in real life?
- Do you make fun of the way people look, talk, dress, or act on a Web site, through text messages, or in a chat room?
- Are you part of a group that does these things—even if you're only being part of the crowd and even if you only look?

If you answered "Yes" to any of these questions, it doesn't have to be this way. Stop causing pain and risking trouble. Become part of the solution instead.

one member flaming a newbie. It happened so much that the moderator contacted the site's owner and complained about the bully. He successfully arranged to have the bully banned from the site.

Enough Is Enough

Even schools are getting into the act. You can be suspended or expelled for cyberbullying. You might think schools can't do anything if the bullying takes place off school grounds. That used to be somewhat true, but no more. In 2007, the Bullitt County, Kentucky, school board decided it was fed up with cyberbullies. Some kids were scared to go to school because of cyberbullying.

The school board was told of several incidents of threats on social networking sites. During the month of January, several hundred students had stayed home from school for one or more days. The school board's lawyer said that at Bullitt Central High School, "the threats had caused a lot of fear among the students that passed on to the parents, and a lot of times the parents would come and remove the students." So now Bullitt County schools are operating under a zero-tolerance policy: If the cyberbullying disrupts the learning process, students can be immediately suspended or expelled, even if the bullying happens off school grounds.

Something similar happened in Canada in 2007. Teachers, parents, and others kept hearing reports of cyberbullying among Canadian teens. They got sick of

How often do you use the Internet to help with your school work? If caught cyberbullying, you could lose your Internet privileges at school or even be expelled.

it and pushed for a change in the law. Now, even when a cyberbully operates from a computer at home, online attacks against other students or even teachers will lead to suspension or expulsion from school.

Too Late for Regrets

Getting busted for cyberbullying can lead to some pretty unpleasant penalties. But you know what the worst punishment can be? It's how you might feel if things go too far. Your own guilt can really do you in. That's what happened to a teen in England. He had bullied his own best friend. He was angry at his friend for drawing embarrassing pictures of him as a joke and showing them to friends. So he decided to make his friend pay. He invented an online character named Callum and put his profile up on the social networking site Bebo. Callum started a relationship with the victim. He got really personal and

Many school boards are tackling the issue of cyberbullying. They are making it an offense with serious consequences even if the bullying happens away from school grounds.

Cyberbullying can cause a lot of pain—for the victim and also for the person doing it.

intimate. Callum pretended to fall in love with the victim. When the boy found out that Callum was a hoax, he fell apart. He had revealed his deepest secrets to Callum, and those secrets had been passed around the school. The victim tried to commit suicide by swallowing 60 pills.

The teen who invented Callum was arrested and tried for harassment. But for him, that wasn't the worst part. The truly awful part was knowing he had almost killed his friend. In court, he said, "I know what I did was really bad but I didn't want anything like this to happen. I am just really sorry." Sometimes the worst consequence of being a cyberbully is the deep regret.

> "I know what I did was really bad but I didn't want anything like this to happen. I am just really sorry."

CHAPTER four

STOPPED BEFORE IT STARTS

Most thinking people agree: The best way to deal with cyberbullying is to prevent it from happening in the first place. Society needs to act. Schools need to act. And kids aren't exactly helpless either.

Several states have adopted cyberbullying laws. These laws spell out the penalties for cyberbullying or require schools to have an anti-cyberbullying policy.

If cyberbullying is taken seriously, officials say, people will think twice before they do it. Stiff penalties could scare people away from cyberbullying. At least that's the hope. It may be awhile before anyone knows how well it works, because most of these laws are new.

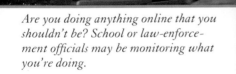

Are you doing anything online that you shouldn't be? School or law-enforcement officials may be monitoring what you're doing.

In some states, cyber threats are covered by general laws against bullying and electronic harassment. In Virginia, for example, Chad ended up in juvenile court. He had IMed his buddies with threats against a former girlfriend. Chad got nailed because Virginia makes cyberbullying a criminal act

It's the Law

Cyberbullying laws already exist in some states. These include Arkansas, Delaware, Florida, Idaho, Illinois, Iowa, Maryland, Minnesota, Missouri, New Jersey, Oregon, South Carolina, Vermont, and Washington. Other states, including New York and Rhode Island, are considering such laws.

when it involves a threat. Virginia's law is called Harassment by Computer. It makes it illegal to use a computer or computer network to "coerce, intimidate, or harass any person." That basically means no scaring people, no going after people to upset them, and no bullying or threatening them. The law applies to both adults and kids. Punishment is up to a year in jail and fines. Chad was transferred to a different school and was ordered to do community service. Virginia legislators hope penalties like this send a message to other would-be cyberbullies.

Other states have laws that deal with phone and computer bullying, too. Most of them make cyber abuse a misdemeanor with punishments of fines and up to a year in jail. In Colorado, you can't annoy, alarm, or harass anybody by phone or computer. Connecticut has similar laws. Pennsylvania makes it illegal to send repeated messages anonymously. In some states, such as Maryland, you can't send lewd

Laws differ from state to state, but in some places, you could serve jail time for cyberbullying by phone or computer.

material to someone if you are doing it to harass them. Former Missouri State Senator Harry Kennedy says that electronic harassment laws are "definitely a warning shot for those folks who want to use the Internet for harassment." And former Missouri Governor Matt Blunt says the laws are protections against criminals and bullies.

Ignorance = Cyberbullies

But do threats like these really prevent cyberbullying? After all, there are laws against stealing,

Remembering Megan

In June 2008, Missouri enacted a new state law making cyberbullying illegal. The law is a response to the tragedy involving 13-year-old Megan Meier. Megan hanged herself in 2006 after being tricked by a false profile on MySpace. She had thought she was friends with a boy named Josh. Then Josh attacked and told her the world would be better off without her. Megan couldn't handle it. Later the mother of one of Megan's so-called friends was accused of making Josh up and signing him up on MySpace. The public was outraged that an adult would cyberbully a child. But Missouri, where the mother and Megan's family lived, had no laws to charge the mother with a crime. In 2008, California federal prosecutors decided to act instead. They charged the mother with computer fraud for lying about her age and name when she signed up at MySpace, which is headquartered in California. She has pleaded not guilty. There is no other way to charge her or anyone else for Megan's death. Fraud was the best the government could do. If such cyberbullying occurs in the future, however, Missouri prosecutors will be able to act.

but people still do it. Many schools and concerned Internet groups think education is a better way. Lots of schools now have cyberbully-awareness programs. They warn students about the serious penalties when people are caught cyberbullying. They try to raise student awareness of how hurtful cyberbullying can be to victims. And they teach that you shouldn't feel ashamed if you are upset by being cyberbullied. They encourage students to report cyberbullying incidents. School atmosphere can make a difference where cyberbullying is concerned. In a school where students value kindness and accept people as they are, there won't be much bullying going on.

Kids who do bully might be acting out or showing off. Some might be cruel, but most are probably just clueless. They never stop and put themselves in the other person's shoes. Most

Think About the Consequences

Many kids and adults don't realize the damage that bullying can do. "At the major concerns level, the students who are victimized can become very depressed," says cyberbullying expert Nancy Willard. "They're likely unable to study or focus in class and may avoid school, leading to school failure. Some are committing suicide. Some are engaging in school violence."

Some schools are starting the Buddy program to help teach students about the dangers of bullying.

people who watch or help cyber-bullies aren't unfeeling, either. They just can't bring themselves to jump in and help the victim. Maybe they are afraid, or maybe they just don't know what to do or say. If you cyberbully or participate in it or silently watch it, you need to consider its impact. Try some of these tips:

- Imagine what it would be like to have this kind of thing happen to you or your best friend. Really put yourself in the victim's place. Think about how unhappy you would be, how much it would hurt, and what it would be like to be unable to fight back.

- Ask a teacher or guidance counselor if your class can have a discussion about cyber-bullying. Talk about whether it's a problem in your school and why it might be happening. See if people are sick of bullying. Discuss what might be done to make things better.

Making a Difference

California teens Emily and Sarah Buder saw a news story about Olivia Gardner, a teen who was the victim of relentless cyberbullying. Emily and Sarah wanted to help Olivia feel better. The girls wrote letters of support and encouragement to Olivia and then began a letter campaign, asking others to write. (Olivia stayed off the Internet because of the attacks she suffered, so letters were the way to go.) Sarah explained, "We basically just wanted to let Olivia know she's not alone, and there are good people out there willing to support her." The project, named Olivia's Letters, grew quickly. Olivia got more than 1,000 letters from around the world. Olivia says, "They just showed me how much everyone really cares about me. It's wonderful and just lifts my spirits up."

If you're upset with a friend, be a true friend—talk to her face to face.

- Get together with friends, and write a skit about a cyberbully and a victim. Perform your skit in front of the class so everyone can see your ideas about how these people might feel.

- Talk about differences. Is it OK to be different? How do differences add to your school community?

- Pretend someone in your school named X is being cyberbullied. X is so upset that he or she has stopped coming to school. You have been assigned the task of sending X a message that will make him or her feel better. What kinds of e-mails or text messages could you write? What exactly would you say?

- Learn how to handle anger. Everybody gets angry, and that's perfectly OK. You don't have to be scared of it or hide it. Tell someone about your anger. If it's safe, tell the person who made you angry and explain why you are so upset. Communicate when you think someone hurt you. Don't seek revenge and plan sneak attacks. Put yourself in the other person's shoes. Listen and try to understand his or her point of view. Build kindness in yourself, in your school, and among your classmates.

Let's Stand Up, People!

When you come right down to it, kids are the people with the real power to prevent cyberbullying. Some people will always bully just for the fun of it or because they like the power. It's in your hands if you see a cyberbully in action or are watching someone suffer the consequences. You're a bystander, but you sure don't have to just stand by. What can you do? Here are some tips from the experts:

- Don't participate. Not even if the whole school is talking about it. If you laugh at it, you are part of it. Don't read a nasty Web page. Don't look at cell phone photos that are sent to make fun of people.
- Don't forward embarrassing photos or spread rumors online or talk about the cyberbullying at school. Don't pass on a cruel joke to the people on your friends list. Let it end with you.

- If you know the victim, be a friend. Ask him or her to spend time with you, hang out, or play a game. Send friendly e-mails, IMs, or text messages.
- Don't stand by in silence. Get help from an adult at home or at school.
- Print or save any evidence of cyberbullying to share with an adult.
- Speak out and tell the cyberbullies to stop. Say that you think their behavior is wrong, unless it isn't safe to do so.

Even if it's your best friend doing the bullying, there's something you can do. Even if he or she is the most popular, important person in your class, you can stand up for what's right and refuse to go along. You can say no or call it mean. It's a scary thing to do, but if you don't, who will? Cyberbullying is never a joke. Your decision to reject bullying could make the difference.

CHAPTER five

YOU'RE NOT DOOMED—REALLY

All this talk about preventing cyberbullying is great, but what if it's happening to you right now? Do you have to wait for some far-off perfect future? No way. You may feel helpless and alone. But there are steps you can take.

You definitely can figure out who should be feeling badly about themselves. (Hint: It's not you.) And there are things you can do to stop the cruelty.

Blame Game

Many people think they are somehow to blame when they're cyberbullied. Instead of blaming the cyberbullies, they think they are somehow weak, worthless, or deserving of the attacks. These feelings can lead to depression and believing you are helpless to change things. They can make you ashamed to tell anyone what is happening to you.

Instead of blaming yourself, try a new approach. First face the fact that you are being cyberbullied. A good rule is: If it feels like bullying, it is. You have a right to label it truthfully. You don't deserve it any more than you deserve being mugged on the street. Self-doubt is a part of growing up, but save it for the important stuff (like what kind of person you want to be). Don't

Take a Stand: The Megan Pledge

WiredSafety.org wants 1 million kids to take a stand against cyberbullying. The group has created a pledge, named for Megan Meier, the 13-year-old girl who killed herself in 2006 after being cyberbullied. The group hopes the pledge will help other victims and stop cyberbullying in the future.

By taking this pledge:

- I agree to take a stand against cyberbullying, including sharing this pledge with others and asking them to take it, too.
- I agree not to use technology as a weapon to hurt others.
- I agree to "Think Before I Click."
- I agree to think about the person on the other side.
- I agree to support others being cyberbullied and report cyberbullying whenever I find it.
- I agree not to join in cyberbullying tactics or be used by cyberbullies to hurt others.
- I agree to "Stop, Block and Tell" when I am being targeted by a cyberbully and to "Take 5!" to help me calm down and walk away from the computer.
- I agree to be part of the solution, not part of the problem.

let some anonymous creep tell you how much self-esteem you should have. Don't let other kids make your decisions for you. If you feel sad, that's OK. Just don't stop believing in yourself.

Take Back Your Power

You can't stop being hurt. Your distress is serious and real. But you can ignore the bully and move on. You can seek the support of friends, family, and any adults you trust. You can also try some of these tips from experts:

• Don't respond. Most cyberbullies want a reaction. That's what they get off on. So don't play their games, no matter how tempted you are.

• Block the sender. What you don't read can't hurt you.

Though it might be embarrassing or scary, if you are being cyberbullied, you need to tell a trusted adult who can help you.

Better to completely ignore the cyberbully.

- Report to the site or ISP. If the bullying is on the Internet, you can notify the ISP. Or use the report button at the Web site. This creates a permanent record of complaint about the post, message, and the sender. Since cyberbullying is almost always a violation of an Internet site's terms of service, the ISP or Web site may close the bully's account.

- Print or save the evidence. Don't hit delete right away, even if you want to. Either save it or print the cyberbully message first. You might need proof of what was said if the bully won't stop.

Tell Someone

The most important expert recommendation is often the hardest for kids to do—tell an adult. If you are scared or overwhelmed, you really might need an adult's help. You'll probably worry that an adult will make things worse. A group of young people shared why they didn't want to tell their parents if they were cyberbullied. Here are some of the reasons they gave:

- "She was afraid if she told her parents she would get restricted, so [she] didn't want to let them know."

Silence Isn't Golden

Too many cyberbullying victims don't tell anyone who can help. A survey of 1,500 teens revealed that more than 40 percent didn't share what was happening to them with anyone. About 38 percent did tell an online friend. But only 11 percent told a parent, and fewer than 4 percent told a teacher. No wonder so many victims feel alone. You need to tell someone who can do something.

- "They might be scared to tell their parents, because they might say, 'I told you so, I told you not to have that blog.'"
- "If you tell your parents a lot of times they'll want to get involved."
- "They overreact."

It Can Happen to Anyone

Samantha Hahn was National American Miss Teen of 2005. She also was cyberbullied for years. The bullies were a girl who had been Samantha's best friend and a gang of four other girls. Today Samantha travels her home state of New Jersey, championing anti-bullying programs. She says, "The message I pass along is simple: If you are bullied, you are not alone nor do you need to deal with it alone. People are out there who will listen and help. And together we can work for change."

Sound familiar? Those are all legitimate concerns. But maybe you can teach your parents or even the school counselor how to handle it. Some parents don't even know what cyberbullying is. So you might have to explain it to them. And when you do, you'll probably have to urge them not to overreact. You can tell them that advice comes straight from the experts. They urge parents not to overreact. They don't need to punish the victim (you). They don't need to cut off your Internet privileges. They don't even need to make you close your social networking site or blog (although it's OK to talk about the possibility).

Asking for help is not always easy—especially when you're worried how your parents might react. Tell them you need their support and understanding. You don't need them to watch you every second of the day. Offer to do a Google search for your name, too—just to be sure there isn't more out there you weren't aware of. Tell them what kind of actions would help you the most. Ask that decisions about how to solve the problem be mutual ones.

But let's be honest here. If you are being threatened, your parents or school may have to go to the police. If your personal contact information is being circulated around the Web, that's serious

If you're the victim of cyberbullying, do a Google search to make sure there isn't more false information about you online.

and dangerous. The adults in your life need to take action.

Parents can be a lot of help, even when the cyberbullying isn't a crime. One teenager got the best help from her dad. She said, "Some girl in my class emailed me calling me a freak and a loser. It made me feel really depressed because I had other things going on, too, at that time. I told my dad, and he called her up and spoke to her. He told her that I didn't read it yet, that it would crush me, and that she should think before she does anything like that again. Well, she never did it again so I guess it worked."

Sometimes parents can surprise you.

Never Give In

Parents or other trusted adults are especially important if you are feeling really, really depressed or thinking about hurting yourself. Your pain is real, and you need their love and support more than ever.

And if you need counseling to get over being a victim, go for it. Don't let cyberbullies win. Listen to Naomi, a young woman who was a victim. She says, "You have no reason to believe me, but take a leap and trust that this is not the real world. This is school. This

"Things are going to get better because I'll never be defined by just one group of people's opinion of who I am."

structure will never exist again, it will never be possible again. ... Things are going to get better because I'll never be defined by just one group of people's opinion of who I am."

So don't give up. There's help around the corner.

QUIZ

Are you being cyberbullied?

Is it really cyberbullying, and do you need help? If you answer "Yes" to any of the questions below, it's real and too hard to handle alone. Tell someone.

✓ Is someone posting information about you on a Web site without your permission?

✓ Do you get nervous or scared when you see you have new e-mail, text messages, or IMs?

✓ Are you receiving lots of anonymous messages?

✓ Have you found out that you were communicating with someone you thought was someone else?

✓ Are there embarrassing pictures of you posted anywhere online?

✓ Have your secrets or private conversations been shared with others without your permission?

✓ Has someone pretended to be you online or in a text message to other people?

✓ Do you worry about what's wrong with you or think about harming yourself?

✓ Have you tried and failed to get the bullies to stop?

✓ Does it feel like bullying?

GLOSSARY

bigotry — intolerance or prejudice

cyberbullying — bullying through e-mail, instant messaging, in a chat room, on a Web site, or through messages or photos sent on a cellular phone

cyber footprints — trail left behind when you are online

emoticon — facial expression, such as a smiley, drawn with keyboard characters

flaming — hostile and insulting words and verbal fights on the Internet

harass — repeatedly send insulting, critical, or hurtful messages

IMing — instant messaging; exchanging text messages in real time

ISP — Internet service provider; company that provides your access to the Internet

lewd — obscene, indecent, and sexually offensive

moderator — someone given the power by the site administrator to enforce the rules of a forum or discussion board

newbie — anyone new to an area on the Internet

WHERE TO GET HELP

**Adolescent Crisis Intervention
& Counseling Nineline**
800/999-9999
*Young people can call this nationwide
hotline for help with problems such as
bullying, depression, abuse, drug addiction,
and more. The Nineline offers crisis counseling, referrals, and information services to
young people and their families.*

Boys Town National Hotline
14100 Crawford St.
Boys Town, NE 68010
800/448-3000
*Anyone can call the Boys Town hotline
for help with any problem at any time.
Trained counselors are available to help
with questions and difficulties of all kinds.*

i-SAFE Inc.
5900 Pasteur Court
Suite #100
Carlsbad, CA 92008
760/603-7911
*i-Safe is the largest Internet safety site on
the Web. i-Safe can be contacted with
questions about its Web site, informational
materials, which student programs are
available, and more.*

Victim Services
National Center for Victims of Crime
2000 M St. N.W.
Suite 480
Washington, DC 20036
800/394-2255
*Crime victims, including teens experienc-
ing violence or bullying, can contact this
government service for information, bul-
letins, and help in finding local services to
assist them.*

SOURCE NOTES

Chapter 1
Page 5, column 2, line 1: Amanda Lenhart. Pew Internet & American Life Project Parents and Teen Survey. 27 June 2007. http://www.pewinternet.org/pdfs/PIP%20Cyberbullying%20 Memo.pdf

Page 9, column 1, line 8: Suzanne Struglinski. "Schoolyard Bullying Has Gone High-Tech." *Deseret News*. 18 Aug. 2006. 12 Oct. 2008. http://deseretnews.com/dn/view/0,1249,645194065,00.html

Page 10, column 1, line 3: Ibid.

Page 11, sidebar: Robin M. Kowalski, Susan P. Limber, and Patricia W. Agatston. *Cyber Bullying*. Malden, Mass.: Blackwell, 2008, pp. 124-25.

Chapter 2
Page 12, line 14: Joan E. Lisante. "Cyber Bullying: No Muscles Needed." CFK: Connect for Kids. 3 June 2005. 12 Oct. 2008. http://www.connectforkids.org/node/3116

Page 19, column 2, line 5: Rachel Simmons. *Odd Girl Out*. San Diego, Calif.: Harvest, 2003, p. 98.

Chapter 3
Page 21, sidebar: Parry Aftab. "What Everyone Needs to Know About Cyberbullying." WiredKids and the Wired Safety Group. http://209.85.215.104/search?q=cache:L_WC1ROBG7sJ:depts.washington.edu/trio/center/resource/web/cyber.doc+%22what+everyone+needs+to+know+about+cyberbullying%22+aftab&hl=en&ct=clnk&cd=3&gl=us

Page 25, column 1, line 9: "Students to Be Punished for MySpace Postings." *Louisville News*. 16 Aug. 2007. 12 Oct. 2008. http://www.wlky.com/news/13897653/detail.html

Page 27, column 2, line 4: Murad Ahmed. "Cyber Bully's Sex Hoax Led Friend to Try to Kill Himself." *Times Online*. 30 Jan. 2008. 12 Oct. 2008. http://www.timesonline.co.uk/tol/news/uk/crime/article3272992.ece

Chapter 4
Page 30, column 1, line 2: "State Harasssment Laws That Explicitly Address Electronic Communications." CyberStalking, Freedom Forum. 12 Oct. 2008. http://www.freedomforum.org/packages/first/cyberstalking/stateharassmentlaws.htm

Page 31, column 1, line 5: "Mo. Lawmakers Vote to Bar Internet Harassment." Associated Press. First Amendment Center. 19 May 2008. 12 Oct. 2008. http://www.firstamendmentcenter.org/%5Cnews.aspx?id=20070

Page 32, sidebar: Cindy Long. "Silencing Cyberbullies." *NEA Today*. May 2008. http://www.nea.org/neatoday/0805/feature2.html

Page 33, sidebar: Jim Staats. "Mill Valley Sisters' Letter Project Bolsters Bullying Victim." *Marin Independent Journal*. 20 April 2007. 12 Oct. 2008. http://www.marinij.com/marin/ci_5710717

Chapter 5
Page 39, column 2, line 8: *Cyber Bullying*, p. 92.

Page 40, sidebar: Samantha Hahn. "Bullying and Cyberbullying: Samantha's Story." *Net Family News*. 12 Oct. 2008. http://www.netfamilynews.org/samantha0510.htm

Page 42, column 1, line 4: "Share Your Story." Cyberbullying.us. http://www.cyberbullying.us/shareyourstory.php

Page 42, column 2, line 9: *Odd Girl Out*, p. 258.

Fiction

Anderson, Mary Elizabeth. *Gracie Gannon: Middle School Zero*. Windsor, Calif.: Rayve Productions Inc., 2008.

Beard, Candy J. *Please Don't Cry, Cheyenne: A Story About Bullying and Friendship*. Frederick, Md.: PublishAmerica, 2007.

Heneghan, James. *Payback*. Toronto, Ont.: Groundwood Books, 2007.

Knapp, J. Richard. *Bobby's Story—Bullies Beware the Power of One*. Parker, Colo.: Thornton Publishing, 2006.

Tassell, Brad. *Don't Feed the Bully*. Santa Claus, Ind.: Llessat Publishing, 2004.

Wilson, Jacqueline. *Bad Girls*. New York: Delacorte Books for Young Readers, 2001.

Nonfiction

Breguet, Teri. *Frequently Asked Questions About Cyberbullying*. New York: Rosen Publishing Group, 2007.

Gardner, Olivia, Emily Buder, and Sarah Buder. *Letters to a Bullied Girl*. New York: Harper Paperbacks, 2008.

Gumm, Merry L. *Help! I'm in Middle School ... How Will I Survive?* Douglass, Kan.: NSR Publications, 2005.

Newman, Matthew. *You Have Mail: True Stories of Cybercrime*. New York: Franklin Watts, 2008.

Simmons, Rachel. *Odd Girl Speaks Out: Girls Write About Bullies, Cliques, Popularity, and Jealousy*. Orlando: Harcourt, 2004.

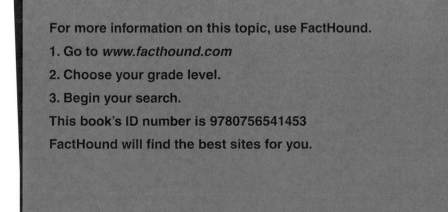

For more information on this topic, use FactHound.

1. Go to *www.facthound.com*

2. Choose your grade level.

3. Begin your search.

This book's ID number is 9780756541453

FactHound will find the best sites for you.

INDEX

ABOUT THE AUTHOR

Toney Allman holds a bachelor's degree in psychology from Ohio State University and a master's degree in clinical psychology from the University of Hawaii. She worked in child development, psychometric testing, and counseling with families for many years in Hawaii. Today she lives in Virginia and has written more than 30 nonfiction books covering a wide variety of topics from Internet safety to diseases to media issues that affect students.

ABOUT THE CONTENT ADVISER

Billy AraJeJe Woods has a doctorate in psychology, a master's in education, and a bachelor's in psychology. He has been counseling individuals and families for more than 25 years. He is a certified transactional analysis counselor and a drug and alcohol abuse counselor. A professor of psychology at Saddleback College, Mission Viejo, California, Woods teaches potential counselors to work with dysfunctional families and special populations. He began his counseling career in the military where he worked with men and women suffering from post-traumatic stress disorder. In his practice, Woods has worked with many young adults on issues related to drug and alcohol abuse and body image.